ALSO BY JEFFREY CYPHERS WRIGHT

Translust

Employment of the Apes

Charges

Two
(with art by Yvonne Jacquette)

Take Over
(introduction by Allen Ginsberg)

All in All
(preface by Alice Notley)

Walking on Words

Drowning Light

Flourish

The Name Poems

October Centerfold
(with art by Nathaniel Hester)

Triple Crown, Sonnets

Party Everywhere

Radio Poems

3-ZERO, Turning Thirty
Editor, (with Elinor Nauen)

Over the Years, Oral Histories from Harlem
Editor

BLUE LYRE

poems by

JEFFREY CYPHERS WRIGHT

J. C. Wright

DOS MADRES

2018

DOS MADRES PRESS INC.
P.O.Box 294, Loveland, Ohio 45140
www.dosmadres.com   editor@dosmadres.com

Dos Madres is dedicated to the belief that the small press is essential
to the vitality of contemporary literature as a carrier of the new voice,
as well as the older, sometimes forgotten voices of the past. And in an
ever more virtual world, to the creation of fine books pleasing to the
eye and hand.

Dos Madres is named in honor of Vera Murphy and Libbie Hughes,
the "Dos Madres" whose contributions have made this press possible.

Dos Madres Press, Inc. is an Ohio Not For Profit Corporation and a
501 (c) (3) qualified public charity. Contributions are tax deductible.

Executive Editor: Robert J. Murphy

Illustration & Book Design: Elizabeth H. Murphy
www.illusionstudios.net

Cover design & author photo: Lori Ortiz

Typeset in Adobe Garamond Pro & Chaparral Pro
ISBN 978-1-939929-96-9
Library of Congress Control Number: 2017956409

First Edition

ACKNOWLEDGMENTS

Blue lyre is a colloquial term for
blue lyre-leaf sage, *Salvia lyrata.*

The author gratefully acknowledges the publishers and
editors of the magazines where some of these poems first
appeared: *Big Hammer, The Café Review, CLWN WR, East
Village Eye, Empty Mirror, Evergreen, First Literary Review-
East, Hanging Loose, Live Mag!, Local Knowledge, New
American Writing, The New Verse News, Nostrovia, OccuPo-
etry, The Otter, Poets Reading the News, Poetrybay, Post Blank
Zine, Reality Beach, Recours au Poéme, Spillwords, Tribes
Magazine, Urban Graffiti,* and *Whitehot Magazine.*

Poems have also appeared in these anthologies: *Brevitas;
Estrellas en el Fuego* (*Stars in the Fire*), and *Palabras Luminosas,*
both from Rogue Scholars Press; *Before Passing,* published
by great weather for MEDIA; and *From Somewhere To
Nowhere: The End of the American Dream* published by
Autonomedia.

"Dare to Be Fun" was published as a broadside by Lunar
Chandelier Press.

"Hecate's Gate" was published as a broadside by Green Kill.

Translation of Sextus Propertius by Vincent Katz

Many thanks to Michael C. Anton, Sanjay Agnihotri, Vyt
Bakaitis, Stephen Betts, Luigi Cazzaniga, Lynne DeSilva-
Johnson, Bill Evans, Ron Kolm, Kimberly Lyons, Shelley
Miller, Rick Mullin, Barbara Rosenthal, Ilka Scobie,
Michele Somerville, Mark Statman, Barry Wallenstein,
Bruce Weber, and Cindy Hochman of "100 Proof" Copy-
editing Services. With special gratitude to my dear family
and a shout-out to the merry crew. And with a bow to the
late Mark McCawley, editor of *Urban Graffiti.*

for Lori

Table of Contents

I BULLETPROOF POEMS

1 ... Haymaker
2 ... The Seer; or, How to Write
3 ... Bare Season
4 ... August's Maw
5 ... Easy Does It
6 ... Meme Quarry
7 ... Gluing Time to the Weather
8 ... Hecate's Gate
9 ... Wounded Star
10 ... Whippersnapper Express
11 ... It's a Mad World After All
12 ... Capacity City
13 ... Mind Your Business
14 ... Staggering Love
15 ... Word of the Day
16 ... Recipe for a Precipice

II COME-ONS

19 ... Dare to be Fun
20 ... Full of Bad Ideas
21 ... Pipe Up
22 ... Petal River
23 ... Around the Bend
24 ... Bumble
25 ... Let's Do Something
26 ... Finally
27 ... Heave-Ho

28 ... Smoke Transfer

29 ... Thimblerig

30 ... Titania's Tool

31 ... Silver Tusk

32 ... Wake-Up Call

33 ... Maroon

34 ... Origin of the Specious

35 ... Prisoner of Bohemia

III ODIN'S WISHBONE

39 ... Begging For It

40 ... Lost In Spades

41 ... Crest

42 ... Free Time

43 ... Command Z

44 ... Boutonnière

45 ... The Mission

46 ... Sam Cooke Book

47 ... Stuntin'

48 ... Folding the Light

49 ... Bells & Whistles

50 ... Thanksgiving; or, Tompkins Square Nobility

52 ... Four O'Clocks

53 ... (B)utterfly

54 ... Runaway Doors

59 ... Poembot

IV SACRED CRUMBS

63 ... Blue Lyre

64 ... White Vulture

65 ... Roaming Charges

66 ... Last of the Mojitos

67 ... Training the Wind

68 ... A Mix of Sun and Clowns

69 ... Damn Skippy

70 ... Rain Dancer

71 ... For Better or Worse

72 ... Crime and Punishment

73 ... "Gone"

74 ... Holiday Gold

75 ... Hands Up

76 ... Gryphon

77 ... Lonely Altar

78 ... Memorizing the Future

81 ... About the Author

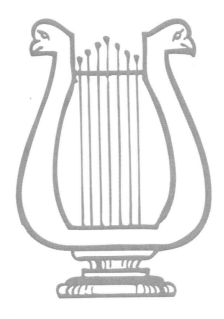

I

BULLETPROOF POEMS

"This fire all there is ... to find ... I find it
You have to find it."

—Alice Notley

HAYMAKER

July raves, deliriously green.
The feverfew stands three feet tall!
Its yellow faces ringed with white

ruffs. A songbird perches in a birch.
Its wings, still when it sings.
How your heart is, inside mine.

We thread our loom with echoes,
a fly buzzing against the screen,
thunder talking to the snails
who write it all down in silver lines.

THE SEER;
or, HOW TO WRITE

for David Meltzer
1937-2016

In the beginning was breath
sounding in the throat.
Shells of words seethed,
breaking on meaning's shore.

If at first you can't write a line,
send for the juggler.
Read the menu and drool.
Something will come to you.

The moon turns to wax,
glowering over North Beach.
When I was a poet
I juggled glowing worlds.

Death, I lived to cheat.
In the beginning was a beat.

BARE SEASON

The late Jim Brodey once instructed me
on composing a New York School poem:
"Use *blue* and name a couple friends."
This off-the-cuff take is on-the-button.
Here's Larry Fagin in *Complete Fragments:*
"Brodey's flashing bolt.
Yellow-pink-red-blue-green-black...."

Here's the deal. Just wow. That's it.
Ratchet the vernacular like the dickens
with Hippolyte mincing beside you.
Popinjay. Nincompoop. Ninny. Dolt.
Poppycock. Rubbish. Return to the fold.
For starters, try kicks, see what you get.
Rain hammers blue nails into dusk's chest.

AUGUST'S MAW

We find ourselves in August's maw.
It's a month to rest but I'm restless.
An Eastern Comma flutters by.
White peaches are in season.
Sweet in the mouth,
they mock my uneatable words.
Red sunset combs a part
in the sycamore's leaves,
knitting shadows that whisper,
"We are getting longer. Are you?"
Fingernail moon grins, complicit.
Night's silence is actually a thousand
cicadas making their opera roar.
A shooting star isn't sleeping either.

EASY DOES IT

We have nothing
to fear
but global warming,
overpopulation,
oligarchy, and getting
fat. I dreamed
my old girlfriend
came back and
we got it on.
That's not happening.
Oh, I'm getting
screwed, all right.
Flood insurance
starts as low
as $200 a year.

MEME QUARRY

You who have a date with Fury,

set the record straight.

The rug is being pulled out

from under the planet.

You must rob the messenger.

Listening to The Highwaymen.

Come, let us away.

Pegasus waits in the wings.

Make mine a Sandman.

Make mine a bedtime story.

Go tell it on the rocks.

DANGER AHEAD

Flirting with extinction,

I'm stickin' with the Union.

GLUING TIME TO THE WEATHER

So exciting I have to forgive myself,
exhale like Moby Dick.
Grace makes me blush.
Here is Ajax with the stuff
as from a black skiff on an endless sea.
As through a veil of candle wax.
I believe in the pile-up of loss,
light shivering inside,
sputtering like a cold engine
fuse-boxed to the disappointment.
A core of silver ringtones.
Pearls stranded by rotting ice.
No excuses for caring so much
as your mouth drops open and jams.

HECATE'S GATE

Betwixt the witching hour's spell
and Happy Hour, I dwell.
Forever halfway home—
between Elysium and delirium.
Slow lightning caught in a zipper.

Your hand shakes in the checkout line.
I vow to be a better boyfriend.
We rob Wells Fargo in my dream.
Duty and purpose direct us
toward the Leopard Colony.

You've put me on the spot, Hecate,
keeping me here, stuck in your transom.
I know you won't let me through,
but I'm going to stay here 'til you do.

WOUNDED STAR

You're always going on
about how unfair things are,
how the deck is stacked for some.
Damn the dealer.
Every whine is one less win.
Let's hear it for the kiss of hell.

Here's to the drowning rat.
Here's to the patrol that's cut off.
Here's to the crippled acrobat.
We're all acting our parts;
I'm wind in a jug,
you're a little off-key.

What could ever take your place?
A grain of salt? A wounded star?

WHIPPERSNAPPER EXPRESS

"I know Zadie Smith.
Her husband's an Irish Wolfhound.
You have no idea.
Where my labia and libido meet,
night unfolds its tent.
I think about fate and deep shit,
rolling around in Bushwick.

To die for love and the resistance,
Eros erasing us with arrows.
Red stuck in gold's keyhole,
pinned to a flame.
Bells licking the sky.
So, the thing is, we have a tie.
It's always like that sometimes."

IT'S A MAD WORLD AFTER ALL

Drought. Fire. Heat wave. Flood.
JUSTIN BIEBER BUSTED FOR POT
Hang on to what we've got, Hope Ranger.
Don't let the bedbugs bite, beautiful
headbanger. By the time you read this,
there will be a million new mouths
to feed. And a million less bees.
Look for me in Shangri-La-La Land.
I'll be the one who's carrying on.
Do yourself a favor. Write a bullet-
proof poem to prove you hear God
and what's left of nature, fellow
dream peddlers. Don't take no shite
—and love your enemies' wives.

CAPACITY CITY

for Ron Kolm

Sure, take the hospital and make a condo.

Luxury spinoff FUBU movement.

Track your tears on the typhoon index.

Cry me a river, bitches, and get up in arms.

I see you where you live, hero decay alarms.

America printed on a mirage.

Strife grifters on the runway strafed.

Momma said the thrifty thrive.

Vigilant is visible; make your sign:

99% AND WON'T LIE DOWN

Strike force under spring fire.

The Shins are playing tonite.

Spokes of the sun spinning backwards.

Let this poem bite the tongues of darkness.

MIND YOUR BUSINESS

The astronauts were weeping
—David Shapiro

Together we've singed night's black wing.
Together we've wrecked the train.
Too many of us—blue drag—
smokestack hurricanes. Futile
fuses for the few, we unresigned poets
shovel love letters into furnaces.
Keep the motor running, Hotfoot.
SKIPPING OVER DAMAGED SECTION
All the hubbub will you nothing buy.
Hubba hubba!
Mug the sun, steal the light.
Let dragons lick your burning tears.
Stop global warming, Camp Fire Girl.
That's your job now, what you're here for.

STAGGERING LOVE

Fluctuat nec mergitur
—the motto of Paris

How cheap blood is, running in the streets.

How naked is aggression,

selling its garments to buy a weapon.

How high is the high ground

when the flood is a sea of faces?

When a sandstorm fills the sandbox.

How shall we all get along?

Relics of the bone codex.

The days grow shorter, while night

grows a long beard.

We are all "bull" fighters now,

managers of staged danger.

Don't point a finger at your neighbors.

Slay stray dragons with staggering love.

WORD OF THE DAY

Faience:

A delicate pale buff earthenware body.

Me too, I'll have some of that.

Quack in the spamiverse.

Hold on to your quiver

and leggo your ego.

We need your help.

Stop mountaintop removal.

Stop robbing the sun's grave.

Call the true pretenders—

surrender to their heirs.

Echo the lucky stars:

Doors open when you least expect it.

Postponing eternity again.

RECIPE FOR A PRECIPICE

for Elaine Equi

Start with overbearing delight,
untenuous joy,
a dash of rectified éclat.

Smoothbore lightning salvaged
from the haunted mirror district.

Blot up a dram of spilled sun,
capturing ruptured rapture.

Stir in a cageful
of moth-eaten shadows.

Add blue snapdragons,
blood squeezed from a Swatch,
mix well and tie into a knot.

In my log of useless beauty,
love has no room for pity.

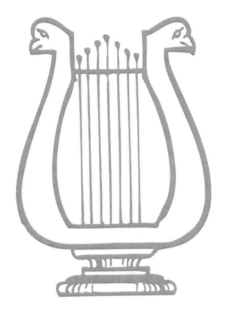

II

COME-ONS

O utinam magicae nossem cantamina Musae!
Haec quoque formoso lingua tulisset opem.

"If only I knew the incantations of the Muse of magic!
This tongue also would bring aid to a beau."

—Sextus Propertius

DARE TO BE FUN

Crows cackle in their gimcrack
cadences, calling all at once.
Oblivious to cold or getting old.
Oblivious to decadence.

White whiskers and rye whiskey
(and a little punch from Judy).
"Just a taste." The wind is doing
a duet with a dumpster

to see which one is louder.
I used to love a banshee,
but now I love the banished.
Wired to the sun.

Lighting the *wick* in *wicked*.
Promise you'll come back here.

FULL OF BAD IDEAS

Here's to Q and A.
Here's to T and A.
Here's to getting back
to our drinking.
Here's to wet gods.
Here's to Confession #87.
Here's to the 6th
missing shore I have
stepped away from.
Here's to the Anti-genius
Museum. Lust is
a firefly in an inferno.
Here's to you.
Inscribe the embers.

PIPE UP

Take me to your swamp thing,
guilt potential. Lay me down
beside pirate-wink sorcery.

Snow cherries hopped up on gris-gris,
park your tongue on my telephone
pole and log on to destiny surge.

Sugar fire-jumper—earn it
the hard way, hammer theater.
Smooch jockey in the hoosegow.

Under your hair: smoking wings,
a moment of beige silence
that nuzzles my puzzle piece.

Like sunlight on the windowpane
you move through me, a gold chain.

PETAL RIVER

Blonde October streaming ash
under glass—how many rooms
your light fills without fail.
Naked under folded wings,
your eyes lace the wind.
The gravedigger's lantern,
exiled by your laughter.

Run to me, oh *arriviste*,
as before. Push me to the wall,
angel fucking a clown.
Let me drift like a petal
on a forking river.
Here we are again ...
in the middle of forever.

AROUND THE BEND

Mercy for those who lie,
finding strength in ambiguity.
Sweet Old Flame,
one jump short of a straitjacket.
INSTAGASM
Clowns slow-dancing for peace.
Wrapping words in bandages.
Destiny, your best friend, crying
silver buckets of yeah, yeah, yeah.
You and me on the same
racehorse in different dreams.
INSTRUCTIONS: Hold out.
Movie night at the lighthouse.
You put the *always* in *forever.*

BUMBLE

Extracting pollen reverb
from your "keep trying
hard" and those who don't
say hello at the Miami Art Fair.
Only the stars can get away
with being dim.
I heard you knocking
on the rocket door.
Here's the rule:
First you ferment
and then you distill.
To sting is to die.
To fly from loosestrife
to bachelor's buttons, that's life.

LET'S DO SOMETHING

Let's do something together
as the future recedes.
How low is the bar?
Make some noise!
It's a serial pleasure to be here.
Plummet bulge assume kerplooey.
You know you've said that before.
Wait, there's more to the story:
A patchwork of kindlings
where we shared a border—
how you wanted to remember it
before it happened,
teetering on the edge
of Heartbreak Ridge.

FINALLY

There was nothing left to say.
Your mouth was a bucket
of hurt. Throngs of diphthongs
stole through your brain
like thieves in a dark
abandoned lot where you
looked for your keys,
metonymically speaking.
And for this a black sheep
they want to brand you?!
Greetings, good-looking.
I know where you can park
your heart and count to three.
You can be a captive of glee.

HEAVE-HO

Keep the change and don't.
No one can stop you anyway.
Minnie Mouse, let's get rowdy.
Josephine Baker, *je t'aime!*
Grenache spills from my cup.
The governor of Missouri
declares a state of emergency
after all-time record floods
slam the Meramec River.
El Niño weds Global Warming.
Help is on the way.
Foreplay on the floor.
Harriet Tubman on drums.
Let's call ourselves The Uh-Ohs.

SMOKE TRANSFER

You are burning in the key
of B major, full out,
orange teeth sawing down
trees and nipping at
a crowded sky—a sky
awash with smudged maps
leading to a palace of ash.
You're unable to contain
the conflagration eating time.
No one cries so beautifully
as they are consumed,
my stand-alone action figure.
Smoke gets in my eyes
watching you ruthlessly shine.

THIMBLERIG

Hottest day of summer,
the neighbor's making pancakes.
Black plums from Madame X
conspire on the sill.
I listen to "new" classical music,
making potato salad.
Up to page 77.
Following the choir.
Listening to the "new" air sound.
Looking for a "new" word order.
I go out and buy some white wine
for tonight's organ shine.
Keep the shells moving
as light swindles evening.

TITANIA'S TOOL

Take me to your navel.
"Aye aye, Capitan."
And you will feel better
in the morning and also
in a few minutes.
After your silk comes off.
After my compass spins.
Ready for the Canon
to come on.
And by the way, your clown
costume becomes you.
"Aye aye, capstan." Let me
hoist you from the depths.
A winch I'll be for my wench.

SILVER TUSK

Consider a ring-tailed shredder,
alone in the corridors of evening,
who presses the moment
against its eyelids. That's me.
Always ready. I can't deny
it's been nice hearing you growl.

Blue drains the waning light.
Snow starting to stick on top
of old wooden water towers.
I think once more of how
your kisses filled the hours
'til I lost score. Zero churn.

Now only ashes remember
how many ways we burned.

WAKE-UP CALL

Married to the sands of time,
a kestrel's rasp rakes
the air in its wake of light.
March pear blossoms arch
over idle side streets,
intersecting without end.
In unblazed sections
where night lingers,
startled seconds stir
at the corner as if you were
living here still.
A red curtain rises.
Morning's face catches fire.
I, too, raze a ghost inside.

MAROON

Marooned angels riddle the sky.
The window wears whiskers
of rain. I have to go out soon
to an opening in Williamsburg
to help my friends defeat death.
My umbrella is doomed.
We are all in this together alone.

About last night ... the ghost ship
responded to our probe.
Forgive me for letting you lead me
astray, to revel in your vessel.
Radio Neptune, asking for clearance.
I can't lie—my lips chased yours
all around the mulberry bush.

ORIGIN OF THE SPECIOUS

Don't give me those woof-woof eyes,
that Dark & Stormy look at KGB Bar,
where sharks offer swimming lessons.
Don't hurt yourself trying to be
like me (although it couldn't hurt).
Don't put lipstick on a ghost.
Never collide with a kaleidoscope
or have a cow if you get a bum steer.
Don't "harbor a grudge";
the water isn't deep enough.
Don't give up. Keep licking night
'til it gleams like sweating jet.
I dreamed a green star rose high
on our left. Don't hold your breadth.

PRISONER OF BOHEMIA

Reporting to the doghouse now, Sir.
DAMAGED GOODS
In love with the Loser Squad.
"You can make it if you try," sings Sly.
"All together now."
Living inside each other.

My poetry, a trap for emotions,
a way station for wayward devotion,
a paradigm shift where heaven waits,
a death-defying praying mantra
looking for the pause button,
my left eye mirroring an eclipse.

My wealth, a bone in Smoke Town.
My faith, a bitch, nips at Sirius.

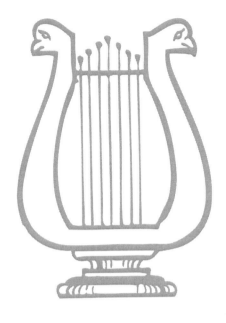

III

ODIN'S WISHBONE

BEGGING FOR IT

O Muse, you vibrate so
rarely. Tune my fork.
I'm but the shell of a note.
A dragonfly's eyelids
fanning the seconds.
A spider's skinny skein
slung from a thorn.
A page's roots clutching
afternoon's passing boat.
I pick up some words
and toss them in the air
to see if you pay any mind.
Just to see
if your breath catches fire.

LOST IN SPADES

Lawnmower grinds day's bones.

Fumes of cut grass slap Campos Plaza.

Two old guys swap banter at the gym,

"Give my regards to Sid Caesar."

They commiserate about fallen arches.

Stand up for the fallen.

Ecco Domani

May rolls out a white carpet

of fallen crabapple blossoms.

Last night, you hid a key in my dream.

Far from court, I stare at the river,

stale and restless in its gray sweater.

Weary and wary of false friends,

Odin's wishbone turns to jade.

CREST

My glass leaves a ring on the tabletop:
dirty looks and mumble-grumbling.
Between blades of grass and thistle,
ajuga's purple cheeks simper.
Common speedwell guards
the driveway, red-violet spikes—
centurions flashing time's dice.
I wonder what is to become
of us, spear hearts …
a pair of spirits bound fast,
tumbling through space.
August's train crests the knoll.
Too late now to worry about the bill.
The Solomon's seal has lost its white cap.

FREE TIME

Sky in puddle looks up to itself,
a pearly patch on the corner.
November dresses in drizzle.
I float on a river of umbrellas.
A band of sycamore leaves
stitches yellow into umber.
A brown penny spins.
A mother's brown eyes glaze
over, stalking the future.
My words pour out, jewels
owned by air, joining raindrops
to be stranded like a necklace
in an old spider's web.
Sky in puddle looks up to itself.

COMMAND Z

Breath's white claw rips apart the air.
With the ache of cold comes clarity.
First frost brings a gray hair.
The mirror is amused. *Et tu?*
It happens overnight. I've seen it all,
you reckon, the blue screen
flickering. Resigned, looking back—
the high-water mark is darker black.
EXIT LEFT
Open season on nature.
What's left to give away?
Conviction will never run out on me.
This is where my life has led.
In my crystal ball, all you see is crystal.

BOUTONNIÈRE

for Miguel Algarín

The gods of Vodka River declare,
Death shall have no sway here,
my little problem child. My boutonnière.
At the Ding Dong Lounge on 105th.

Raised up on 6th Street and FDR Drive,
you're always down for cooked peaches
in Newport or San Juan. You regret
that "Men can't say 'chicks' anymore."

Dirty looks—I know them well.
You must be a mold. "In the rear,"
you quip. Our barstools spin.
Lit candles prick night's womb.

Onyx-spectrum, panther driven.
Let's go for a ride together on the Whip.

THE MISSION

for Ronnie Burk
1955-2003

The bear went over the mountain, Ronnie.

Moon-bone. Cosmic hobo. Trickster.

In your diary, tears run from

the faucet. Time drips. A white raven

sifts lightning from your ribs.

The third eye of the ninth fairy winks.

Ronnie, with your Comanche hair,

your black irises flashing code

as you sailed into The Tempest,

the stars dialing 415-643-1843.

That's how the bear called it.

He left a light on when he left the light.

Like you, a product of the revolution,

who gave some heart to the starving gods.

SAM COOKE BOOK

Happy endings are my destination;
whether or not they are my destiny
is different, thank fuck,
or we'd be stuck in neutral
in the here-we-come!
I think I need a new high.
Drill a well in the wilderness.
Dangle-swirl, call me "Butterface,"
dancing on the edge of a carapace.
Gargoyles gargling with bongwater.
Geronimo's birthday present ticking.
A wave of smiles washes over the deck.
Tack to port, *Chéri.*
Repeat after me: "I *am* a lucky duck."

STUNTIN'

Amen comes from *omen*.
You are headed for oblivion,
stuntin' with the imam
in Oman.
Layin' it on the linebacker.
"Loaded for bear," adds Val.
A hawk rests on a cross
on top of St. Nicholas.
Band names:
The Healers,
The Vials.
I'm going to rebrand myself
The Texas Abortion Clinic.
God comes from *guide*.

FOLDING THE LIGHT

… and striking the drum,
this is air, this is flight.
These are god tracks on my head.
Milk from the stars in your eyes,
who bore the chores of love.
Your tongue, a higher authority,
scrubs the mission
to pry apart our private parts.

How do you keep your act together?
Banished by the eight balls,
I walk on a rope blindfolded,
playing house with chipped words.
After the Sherpas leave,
I will let the animals win.

BELLS & WHISTLES

We were hijacking the language …
taking it to an undisclosed locale
where navigation is out the window.

We were following the heart to an
incinerator of warning labels—all
on fire with a desire to be useful.

Much like a monsoon in a canteen.
Contents under pressure. See how this
produces a feeling of stubborn content.

See how it makes us feel—
like an aporia lurking in the center
of our tale at every twist and trace.

See how these words are a necklace
for the page—beads of black solace.

THANKSGIVING;
or, TOMPKINS SQUARE NOBILITY

... an inch of longing's just an inch of ash.
-Li Shang-yin

On padded rabbit paws, November
leaves us gifts of gold and amber.

Crimson, damson, saffron, and plum.
The hawthorn glows—a candelabrum,

its tips with topaz jets lit. Scarlet
pin oaks bleed into russet and rust.

Old elms, a cavernous canopy bestow,
mirrored by orange parquetry below.

Preparing for slumber, redbuds nod under
heavy crowns set with rubies and garnet.

Gingkoes drop lemony fans in heaps.
Bare crabapples have spent their wads.

One lone leaf greets me spinning down
to join its brethren scurrying around

seeking out a corner, a home to find.
In green gloves, a shy locust lags behind.

Or is it you back there, half-vanished
in mist, reminding me of my truest wish.

FOUR O'CLOCKS

I play catch-up
in a hammock.

Wind blends oak and
aspen leaves with lawn

mower, fountain dream.
A pickup on County Road 7.

Branches bend, brush.
Green slides over green,

sibilant, susurrus,
asking, "What's the russsh?"

I lie down
and stare up.

Always the sky
has the last say.

(B)UTTERFLY

The empty field
my sight fills.

Sky, drunk on blue,
stitched by geese.

Sun a bouquet
of knotted yellow,

cloud flowers
stirred in like cream.

A boat glosses
the river—*splash.*

Yeah, well,
my heart's a reed

this poem blows
through.

RUNAWAY DOORS

I

Door scratched out of homemade sky.
Door made of pink tongues
forever telling jokes
to a door of white ash.
Door of my skull etched
into a door of candle wind.
Doors buried under moth dust.
Doors with no business being doors.
Doors without borders.
The war on doors.
A door without a country.
A door that's in a jam.
Runaway doors
swaggering through leftover heaven.

II

Door of tomorrow's marrow

huddled between imposter doors.

Involuntary dream door

exacerbating God's twin.

Old-timey door swimming

through a dive bar.

Door chops.

Door closing between us

because I am impatient,

a snowflake in heat,

and you are impervious,

a door on the edge of a cliff.

Door built by Yeti women.

Ali Baba and the forty dwarfs.

III

Enemy doors growling

with warheads stuck in their gullets.

Door of the shroud maker,

lonely in her needle EYE.

Door to the Department of Nonsense.

Door to the Zero-Clue Zone.

Naked doors screaming with indecision.

Doors fiddling in the clown wing

while thermometers rise with the tides.

VIP doors to nowhere in the hush panic.

Plastic doors lining the ocean floor.

Haunted doors, leering in the flood grate.

A door wanted by law enforcement

for forging my forgotten cell key.

IV

Door hiding in a keyhole.

Door standing in line to lie to Congress.

Last one in line is a doorstop.

Hello, door of last resorts.

Unsustainable door of the insatiable.

Pregnant teenage door.

Two-time loser door.

Door with a rap sheet.

Door that hears your dreams boil.

Door that splits us in half.

A door that is a jar.

A pair of paradoxical doors.

I'm crazy-for-you-door but you're crazy,

crazy door that I adore.

V

Door stealing the door to the future.

A fake door on fire

where your heart used to beat.

An imaginary door with false teeth.

A door begging to be let in.

A red door in a radioactive cage.

A door covered with dry sedge.

A door made of drought.

A hungry door with lockjaw.

If it don't stink, it ain't shit door.

The "nobody cares about you" door.

Petrified doors, dying to escape.

A poor door falling forever behind.

Door you were born to end before.

POEMBOT

for Chris Toll
1948-2012

You find yourself in a jar of night's hair,

plastered to the sky like a reset button

dedicated to illuminating

catastrophe's apostrophe leaving the station.

Writing is thinking of leaping into the abyss.

No exaggeration too big to miss, Chris.

Now you're looking for anterior galaxies

to replicate the pilgrim's dream

you worked so hard to free.

Marble now, my hands

holding your book, *The Disinformation Phase.*

Each page waves, polishing September's lip.

Outside your window, wisteria sighs like

an old bellhop; "This way, sir. Going up."

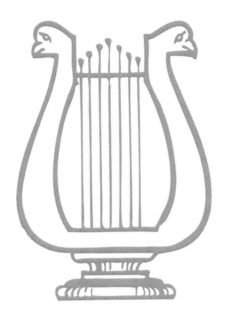

IV

SACRED CRUMBS

"God is love
they say,
in human words."

—Franz Wright

BLUE LYRE

*Whimsical resistance may be more effective
than forms of organized protest....*
—Ted Lawson

Living like a jack-in-the-box,

meeting Luigi at Percy's Tavern at 5,

flipping through Filip's new book.

Half fairy, half wolf.

Pumpmeister of the HIVE DUMP.

Something you keep coming back to

like the future of "Daydream 99."

A first snowdrop pops up.

OCCUPY

As you wish;

let candles do the rest.

On Waverly Place I never waver.

And in the swale, wild blue lyre

opens its lips in a silent choir.

WHITE VULTURE

Grab a red matchbook from KGB.
Grab a picture of Alice and Anne
at Poets House. Lewis and Star.
Mugging with Tod, cap flipped up.
"We are the return address,"
Steve claims at the Cake Shop.
Patricia puts a red dot on the wall.
Miguel says, "Why don't you
stick your finger in his butt."
You call this a sonnet?
What we all cared about. Hungry
puppets licking the wasteland.
In a race with the East,
eat the wind, leave light behind.

ROAMING CHARGES

Go out at night and marry trouble.
Stay in the mix.
Burn up the floor all around.
Try to outfox the future.
Cultivate a vatic avatar.
All roads lead to roaming around.
LMAO
Not your grandmother's meme.

But now I'm stuck here on a tuffet,
impervious to languor's detours,
teasing out time's knots
and scoring hours.
In a race with the erasers,
make every second a first.

LAST OF THE MOJITOS

A clock full of leaves
knocks on my bubble town.
I am not Atlas to haul
time's circling hands around
on my way to the hoodoo palace
to pay my overdue dues.
What kind of monkey
would monkey with *us*?
You again, Mnemosyne,
our ghostly host!?
Accountant of the Now.
Extend your concertina lips.
FINISHING LASTS
White roses falling in slow-mo.

TRAINING THE WIND

I would wear a mantle of blue,
a merlin perched on my arm.
I'd coat the streets with oaths
hunting down your breath
as you gather moon-leaf powder
to dust the stars' spurs with.
You are hard to hold on to.
You burn out of control out west.
You whistle over a bottle's lip.
The trees on South Mountain all
know your name. They say it
only when you come around.
At last, it is almost now again.
You herd cries of the unheard.

A MIX OF SUN AND CLOWNS

Alternating presences inhabit my ...
SKIP AHEAD
Hounded by bounding hours,
I stand at the crossroads
annihilating afternoon,
sticking shadows to the lens.
What did you expectorate?

Must we draw a diaphragm?
Juno in a fishbowl.
The jester also jousts,
pulling strings from the wreckage.
Call me Oracle Fodder—
doing solitary part-time.
Closing in on the opening now.

DAMN SKIPPY

The teepee's not big enough for us all.
Why don't you just go buy something.
I would be a penguin in Hell
and spit at the inferno. By your leave.

Cut me. Wound me. Do your worst.
Put another notch on your pod
in the vanish drift of cooked north,
chopping through the language glut.

Sun Lord. Here is my HELP sign:
SHINE ON ME
Would you rather do the frog march
or the perp walk? This is only a test.

Even if you stand on a deserted speck,
hacking the floor with a speckled axe.

RAIN DANCER

It's raining. Crooked trees
wear the greenest moss.

Every day a lesson sticks,
adding to the stack of needles.

So much currying,
so little favor.

So much scurrying,
just to hold steady.

By the time I get to Phoenix,
I'll be Icarus.

Lord of the wings
in charge of falling.

Rain. Moss, so green.
Today I am all I have given.

FOR BETTER OR WORSE

for Cara and Anders

For richer or poorer,
in darkness or light,
partly sunny or cloudy,
in rain or at night—
may your vows protect you
on the high road or the path,
in tall grass or on the strand,
in a blizzard or a mine.
May your days be directed
by red giants winking,
by ventriloquists of love
and thunder from the gods.
Let no one put asunder
two hearts beating—
one for the other.

CRIME AND PUNISHMENT

That time Mark scarfed down acid
in the back seat of a patrol car
in Naples, Florida. I was 21.
Jayne Anne Phillips rode shotgun.

That time I stole a cardboard nurse
from the Marine recruiting office.
That time I swiped a flag from
in front of the VFW on Cherry Street.

Got 5 days and fined $150 for that
prank. Dad refused to see me.
A friend of his brought a copy
of *Crime and Punishment* to the jail.

That time, late—late in August
when Dad called with the diagnosis.

"GONE"

"Irk" was one of my dad's favorite words.
Mom liked to pick up on teen lingo.
She said "stuff" was "neat."
She was a real people person.
She was chiffon and Dad was concrete.
I walk in the valley where they met.
I walk in a "marijuana haze" (how
Dad put it) in New York City. He was
a quarter leprechaun. She was half elf.
I caused them both a lot of grief.
Had I shown more love, I'd be less bereft.
I walk in ghost shoes, my words
a threnody belonging to the throng.
My folks stay closer now they're "gone."

HOLIDAY GOLD

This day I give to small steps
to make it a special occasion,
to do something nice together.
You want it to linger a little longer,
the last tooth of summer …
a shy breeze cooling your brow.
Oops, I spill your decaf cappuccino.
Laughing, you call me a "klutzatina."
A trumpet player rolls some light
around his horn. A pigeon flies
across the park, landing on his arm.
You point this out and I look up
from my book of flickering wicks:
and see *you*—gold inside of amber.

HANDS UP

This day I give back to salt.
This day, with its whipped miracle.
This day, dragging its dusty tail.
This day in the tiger cage,
alone with a shrinking head.
I dream of fleeing the asylum—
running down steps to nowhere.
This day I chase a bat out of hell.

This day I give to small steps.
I water my jade and red *coleus*.
I contribute to the planet's breath.
This day of long black dresses.
This day of sacred crumbs and
Pekingese on leashes yapping.

GRYPHON

My eyes are green. My beak is quick.

I live on the fringe, ever vigilant.

Pages of a calendar, my wings stir.

I live between Greyhound stops.

My tail can speak but only to lie.

I live on, in unremembered dreams.

My claws ring like stars on an anvil.

I live in a gully, easily provoked,

my heart mimicking an ode to a yoke.

I write poems in letters 100 feet high.

If you ever saw one, you'd probably die.

I live unscathed in distilled wilderness.

My smile is always here, on the horizon

where I live, in an abandoned instant.

LONELY ALTAR

I wish we had more time, is all,
to find our way back across
the bridge of crying snowmen
to say goodbye to the last bee.
Our future, honeycombed
with sacrifices.
It is Sunday in New York.
Everything is perfect,
but not everywhere.
A specter tells the inspector
it was Thor who did it
with a hammer in the foyer.
NAME WITHHELD BY REQUEST
You can't make this stuff up.

MEMORIZING THE FUTURE

Hold tight to the sun's mane.
Practice what you love.
Our job is to level the playing field.
How to get better at beginner's luck?
We all get a "surprise" in the finale.
UPRISE
Rattle the clock.
Plane the day's burl veneer
'til paper-thin curls cover your tracks,
your voicebox humming on a lathe,
burning song into the grain.
No more will I maraud mirages,
maundering along the shoreline.
This isn't really how it ends.

ABOUT THE AUTHOR

 JEFFREY CYPHERS WRIGHT is a publisher, impresario, critic, eco-activist, and artist. He is best known as a poet.

The author first studied with Ted Berrigan, Alice Notley, and Jim Brodey at the Poetry Project, where he later taught and served on the Board. He received an MFA in Poetry after studying with Allen Ginsberg and William Matthews at Brooklyn College, where he also taught.

As a publisher, he's published hundreds of poets, beginning with Hard Press postcards in 1977. From 1987 to 2000, Wright ran a monthly review of all the arts, called *Cover Magazine, the Underground National*. In 2007 he began *Live Mag!*, a journal of art and poetry.

As an impresario and MC, Wright has curated and hosted readings and performances at numerous and varied venues, including nightclubs, community gardens, galleries, St. Mark's Church, and the Bowery Poetry Club.

Wright has written art and poetry reviews for *ArtNexus, Chelsea Now, White Hot, Tribes,* and others. For many years he was a poetry reviewer for *The Brooklyn Rail*. He is now a regular critic for *American Book Review*.

Poems of his are included in the anthologies *Up Late; Thus Spake the Corpse; Out of This World*; and *Aloud*. Currently, Wright stages events in New York City at KGB Lit Bar and at La Mama E.T.C. in conjunction with *Live Mag!*

www.livemag.org
www.jeffreycypherswright.com

For the full Dos Madres Press catalog:
www.dosmadres.com